Winter's Song

Written by Claire Daniel
Illustrated by Leslie Bowman

Dad says, "It's time to sleep now.
But tomorrow you will hear winter's song."

"What is winter's song?" we ask.

"You'll see," Dad says. "Tomorrow, things will be covered with snow. We will hear winter's song."

The next morning, Dad gives us
our coats. He gives us our hats.

"We're going out," he says.
"We're going to hear winter's song."

A big green truck plows the snow.
It turns and comes back. It pushes the
snow up and around.

Rumble, rumble, crash, and bumble!
The truck is playing winter's song.

We get on a sled. Dad gives us a push. Swoosh, swish!

We scream, we yell! We have a lot of fun. Our sleds are playing winter's song.

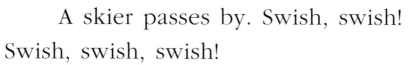

A skier passes by. Swish, swish!
Swish, swish, swish!

She turns and glides. The skier is playing winter's song.

Small birds are looking for their
food. Chirp, chirp.

Scratch, scratch, scratch. Birds are playing winter's song.

We each make a small white fort.

We put green flags on top.

Then we take turns throwing snow.
Split, splat!

"I got you!"

"You did not!"

"Yes, I did!"

"No, you didn't!"

Can you hear us? We are playing winter's song.

It's still snowing. But now it's time
to go to bed.

We look out the window. Things are
all covered with snow.

Can you hear it?

There's not a sound. It's only
the snow . . .

playing winter's song.